LESSONS FROM A SHEEP DOG

PHILLIP KELLER

W PUBLISHING GROUP™

www.wpublishinggroup.com

A Division of Thomas Nelson, Inc.
www.ThomasNelson.com

Library of Congress Cataloging in Publication Data
Keller, W. Phillip (Weldon Phillip), 1920-
  Lessons from a sheep dog.
  1. Border collies—Biography. 2. Keller, W. Phillip (Weldon Phillip), 1920- . 3. Christian life—1960- . 4. Sheep ranchers—British Columbia—Vancouver Island —Biography. 5. Chirstian biography—British Colum-bia—Vancouver Island. 6. Sheep dogs—British Colum-bia—Vancouver Island—Biography. 7. Dogs—British Columbia—Vancouver Island—Biography. 8. Dogs—Biography. I. Title.
SF429.B64K44 1983   280'.4 [B] 82-16124
ISBN 0-8499-0335-1
ISBN 0-8499-3130-4

Printed in the United States of America
01 02 03 04 PHX 20 19 18 17 16 15 14 13

Books by W. Phillip Keller

Splendor from the Sea
As a Tree Grows
Bold under God—A Fond Look at a Frontier Preacher
A Shepherd Looks at Psalm 23
A Layman Looks at the Lord's Prayer
Rabboni—Which Is to Say, Master
A Shepherd Looks at the Good Shepherd and His Sheep
A Gardener Looks at the Fruits of the Spirit
Mighty Man of Valor—Gideon
Mountain Splendor
Taming Tension
Expendable
Still Waters
A Child Looks at Psalm 23
Ocean Glory
Walking with God
On Wilderness Trails
Elijah—Prophet of Power
Salt for Society
A Layman Looks at the Lamb of God
Lessons from a Sheep Dog
Wonder o' the Wind
Joshua—Man of Fearless Faith
A Layman Looks at the Love of God
Sea Edge
Sky Edge
Chosen Vessels
David I
David II

CONTENTS

THE STORY:
Lass—a Beloved Border Collie   *11*
SHEEP DOG LESSONS
Lesson 1
In the Wrong Hands   *29*
Lesson 2
Set Free—to Follow   *43*
Lesson 3
Learning to Trust   *57*
Lesson 4
The Delight of Obedience   *71*
Lesson 5
The Test of Faithfulness   *85*
Lesson 6
Love and Discipline   *99*
Lesson 7
Available for Anything   *113*

The Story

Lass—a Beloved Border Collie

This is a simple story about a special dog who shared life with me on my first sheep ranch. Though she bore the very ordinary name— "Lass"—she was in fact a most extraordinary dog. And my memories of her companionship, loyalty, exuberance and love linger on across the years as joyous, colorful recollections.

Even more important and precious, however, were the powerful, spiritual principles God, my Father, enabled me to learn through working with this beautiful border collie. Some of us are slow to grasp the great basic truths of divine design. We cannot always clearly comprehend Christ's call to us in simple service. For that reason His gracious Spirit often uses the common experiences of life to shed the intense light of supernatural truth upon our path.

It is the basic principle of using parables drawn from our work-a-day world to help us clearly understand the noble, wondrous purposes of our loving Father. This Lass did for me as a young man. I was only in my late twenties when she came into my life. There were searching, burning questions in my spirit then that no sermons or studies had ever resolved for me.

Yet, in His gracious, generous way God used this dog to help me really see what He Himself is like in character and conduct. Beyond that He taught me emphatically what His highest purposes and best intentions were for me as His friend and coworker. For He does make it very clear that as His people, He calls us to special service with Himself.

As a lad I had grown up with cattle. On our land in East Africa, my father had always bred the finest of the breeds adapted to the tropics. His cattle were a special joy to him: the splendid bulls that sired our calves, the sturdy oxen that hauled our wagons and worked our fields, the handsome cows that produced our milk were a marvel to the Africans.

When I came to North America to complete my

14

university training in science and animal husband-
ry, cattle still played an important role in my
career. I worked on various cattle ranches and
longed for the day when I would be in a position to
purchase my own "spread" and establish my own
herd. By my mid-twenties I had been made manag-
er of one of the most beautiful ranches in the inte-
rior cattle country of British Columbia.

There I was given a magnificent, big, cou-
rageous cattle dog named "Paddy." He was excellent with our herd of registered Herefords, and
saved me hours of work in handling the stock.

It was shortly after this that I found a piece of
neglected ranch property on a peninsula of land at
the southern tip of Vancouver Island. Because it
was so abused the place did not attract much interest. But I could see the potential in this land
surrounded by the sea. It was an estate sale, so all
cash had to be paid for the property.

The net result was I had insufficient funds left to
purchase cattle. So I was obliged to start out with
sheep. It quickly became obvious that dear old
Paddy was completely baffled and bewildered by
sheep. So in disgust and dismay he began to resign
himself to snoozing in the sun or sleeping by the
fire.

15

LESSONS FROM A SHEEP DOG

Quickly I realized that I faced a serious dilemma with my first flock. I simply had to find a sheep dog to help me handle the ewes and lambs that grazed on my impoverished pastures. My highest hope was to come across a well-bred border collie. For, of all the breeds, they are the finest sheep dogs.

In passing I might mention that during those initial months at "Fairwinds," for that is what we called our spot by the sea, I began to wonder seriously why I had allowed myself to be "stuck" with sheep. Compared to cattle they seemed so stupid, so timid, so frail, so vulnerable to diseases and parasites, such easy prey to predators.

Little did I then comprehend the wondrous ways of God. Little did I discern His hand at work behind the scenes of my affairs. Little did I realize the enormous, eternal lessons He would teach me on those wind-blown acres where I struggled to make a beautiful country estate out of derelict land.

16 One day there was a short advertisement in the city newspaper. It read very tersely:

"WANTED—A GOOD COUNTRY HOME FOR PURE-BRED BORDER COLLIE.
CHASES CARS AND BICYCLES."

The Story

I hurried up to a neighboring rancher's house and phoned the owner in town, some twenty-seven miles away. "Yes," the lady replied on the phone, "I still have the dog. Please do come quickly. No one else wants her." Her voice sounded desperate.

In short order I drove my old car down the winding country road and pulled up outside a cute little cottage in the city suburbs. The lady was waiting for me at her gate. Almost before I could get out of the car, she came over and began to talk excitedly.

"Mr. Keller, I can't do a thing with this creature." There was a look of anger in her eyes. "The dog is plumb crazy. She's 'loco.'" The woman threw up her arms in dismay. "All she does is tears after the kids; chases boys on bicycles; jumps all the fences and races after every car that comes by on the road."

"Please let me see her," I requested, trying to calm the owner's excitement. "Maybe I can do something with her. I have had dogs all my life."

She led me around to the back of the house. As we entered the little yard, a flying, leaping bundle of dog flung herself toward me. She snarled and snapped, then collapsed in a heap on the ground.

Instantly, to my shock and horror, I saw the dog

was not only chained from her collar to a steel post, but also was hobbled by another, second chain from her neck to her back leg. What a pitiful spectacle!

Crouched in the dirt, covered with dust, the dog glared at me. Her ears were laid back in anger. Deep, guttural, menacing growls rumbled in her throat.

"How old is she?" I asked, my question put to the owner to help cover the profound pity and love that welled up within me. "And what is her name?"

The owner replied that the dog was already two years old, and her name was Lassie.

I looked at the border collie with mingled emotions. She was a dog "gone wrong" . . . totally useless . . . a sad spectacle . . . almost beyond hope, beyond help.

Yet somehow I saw beyond all this. In her eyes I saw a keen intelligence. In her beautiful head I saw a great capacity to learn. She had a splendid constitution with deep, wide chest, broad back and strong legs. The master breeders had done a magnificent job of producing such a superb creature.

With love, compassion and empathy I looked

down at this forlorn, hopeless animal crouched in the dust.

"At two years of age, most dogs have learned all they ever will know," I remarked to the lady, my eyes full of agony. "But she is too beautiful to destroy. I am prepared to give her a chance to change."

The owner was still, tense, waiting for my next words.

"I will take her home to my ranch on one condition." I weighed each word carefully. "If I cannot do a thing with her, after six weeks I will bring her back to you. She is too lovely a specimen for me to put her away. You must then destroy her."

The lady gladly agreed to my proposition.

So I unhobbled Lass (from now on that would be her name). I led her out to my car and put her behind the front seat for the long ride home.

All the way I talked to her softly and reassuringly in a low, gentle voice. All I got in response were low growls. Occasionally I would try to put my hand back to touch or pet her, but she would only bare her teeth and snap back angrily.

I could see why the two years of her town life had been very tough both for her and her owner.

19

LESSONS FROM A SHEEP DOG

Reaching the ranch, I felt a peculiar, inner assurance that somehow this torn and twisted dog would be redeemed. Our land lay at the very end of the country road where it ran into the sea. There were virtually no cars to chase, no boys on bicycles to tempt her, just the wide rolling pastures, the wooded rock ridges and the rugged shoreline where ocean waves thundered against the land.

Most important, there was a new master.

Lass was given a kennel with fresh clean bedding. She had a bowl of sparkling water. A dish heaped with delicious food was placed before her.

She would touch none of them.

She refused to eat, to drink, or enter the kennel.

Every advance made to touch or pet her was rejected.

Any attempts made to call or reassure her were resisted belligerently.

Day followed day. She was beginning to lose condition. And I even began to fear she might die.

In an act of faltering faith I settled on a daring step. I decided to set her totally free. The instant I did so she fled into the forest behind our cottage. In a matter of moments she had disappeared from view. And I wondered if I would ever see her again.

For several days I drove up and down the road

looking for her. I asked other ranchers in the area to let me know if they saw her. But there was no sign anywhere. It was as if she had simply vanished into ocean air.

Then one evening, I happened to glance up at the top of a large rock outcrop behind our home. There, on the summit, Lass lay crouched like a hunted cougar, looking down at me. I called her name, but she turned and fled.

That evening I took food and water and placed them up on the rock for her. At dawn they were gone. So I fed her regularly, but there was no response to any of the overtures I made to her.

A couple of weeks later a small band of sheep grazed near her lookout. Suddenly I noticed she took a keen interest in them. She would cock her head, rise on her haunches and watch them intently. Her latent, inbred instincts were coming to life.

So evening after evening, when the day's work was done, I brought up a few ewes and lambs to graze near where she was.

21

During all this time, though no intimate rapport had been established between Lass and myself, I felt an enormous compassion for this beautiful dog. An intense longing permeated my whole being for her to come to me, to get to know me, to trust me, to learn to love me, to work with me, to be my friend.

Yet, now, week was following week and the time was approaching when she might have to be destroyed. It was an appalling alternative that filled me with dismay.

Then one gentle evening the sun was setting in a golden haze over the ocean. The sheep were grazing contentedly in a lovely pastoral scene at the water's edge. I stood entranced, my hands clasped behind my back, caught up in the wonder of it all. The dog was not really in my thoughts at that moment.

Suddenly I felt a soft warm nose touching my hands.

Lass had come! My heart seemed almost to stop with ecstasy. Elation and ecstatic delight swept through my senses. Contact had been made! She had found the fortitude to let me touch her life.

It was the turning point in our association.

It was the beginning of a remarkable companionship.

It was the start of great adventures together.

Quickly Lass discovered that she had a new master whom she could truly trust. She had come into

22

the care of one who really loved her, who understood her, who had only her best interests in mind.

More than that. She also began to realize that not only did I understand her, but also I knew all about sheep, all about ranching, and all about the exciting part she could play in the whole operation.

On the basis of our mutual affection and trust I began to teach her the common commands so essential for success. Because of her alert mind and fine intelligence she learned very quickly. The familiar phrases and orders such as *"Come"—"Lie down"—"Sit"—"Fetch them"—"Stay"—"To the left"—"To the right"*—were readily understood and soon obeyed.

One aspect of her personality that especially impressed me was the obvious pleasure she derived from doing what I asked of her. Her eyes, large, brown and luminous, would shine and sparkle. Her whole face would be wreathed in a happy smile when I complimented her on her cooperation.

From voice commands, we gradually progressed to silent hand signals, so that even if she was at a great distance from me she understood what to do. She would watch the movement of my right arm and outstretched hand. So she became able to han-

23

dle the sheep with remarkable skill, energy and good will.

As sometimes happens in cases of this kind, word about this remarkable working dog began to spread across the country. Strangers would drive out from the city just for the joy of watching this lovely border collie handle sheep under her master's care. It was a fine compliment to her.

One of the truly touching aspects of our deepening friendship was her utter devotion to me. Where before she had been so shy, so distant, so antagonistic, now she became my virtual "shadow." Where I went, she went. She wanted me always in full view. My presence was her peace and her pleasure.

She became essentially a "one man dog." She would eat and drink only what I provided. She was mine and mine alone.

The skilled breeders of the border counties of England and Scotland had produced this superb strain of sheep dog. All the ancient, inherent instincts for loyal and faithful service came to full fruition in Lass. This was the precise purpose for which she had been brought into being. Now she reveled in that life with abundant energy and exuberant life.

24

The Story

Strange as it may seem, the most difficult command for her to comply with was "Stay." Sometimes it meant that she would have to hold a bunch of lambs in the corner of a field or guard a gate or keep watch over some unruly rams while I was doing another job. It was very trying for her to have me disappear from view. She was always so eager to be where the action was. She wanted to be on the move in the midst of excitement. So she would sometimes be sorely tempted to "break faith" and take off on other tempting escapades.

Two of these were somewhat amusing, yet also posed rather serious problems if we were in the midst of handling the flock. The first was the colony of crows that had their rookery in the stunted, wind-blown trees on a small rocky island just offshore. The black rascals would come winging in over our fields, then swoop down low over Lass to taunt and tease her with their raucous cries.

Unable to restrain herself any longer she would leap to her feet and race away after her tormentors. She seemed literally to fly over the fields, her lithe and graceful body appearing almost airborne in flowing motion. It was a spectacular show and impressive display but it did neither the sheep, the ranch or her master one particle of good.

It was simply a show.

The second cause of her discomfiture were the great land-clearing fires we had in the winter. Sometimes the flaming sparks and glowing cinders carried up and away in the wind were so exciting she would go leaping and bounding after them. Occasionally one would catch in her long lustrous coat and begin to burn with an acrid odor.

Lass would roll wildly in the grass, then shaking herself come racing back to me as if to say: "Well, Boss, wasn't that a great display?" Yes it was, but it had only wasted her energies, sapped her strength and caused her to break faith.

She could quickly sense when I was disappointed. She knew at once when she had let me down. She was fully aware when a coolness came between us because of her misconduct.

There had to be a severe reprimand. There would be a measure of strict discipline. She would have to be taken in hand and corrected for her failure to be faithful in the line of duty.

These were difficult and disagreeable moments for both of us. But they were absolutely essential for her well-being and mine. The entire operation of the ranch and our success with the sheep depended in large measure upon her implicit obe-

26

dience. For by now she had become worth several hired men to me in handling the flock. We were inseparable coworkers.

When the discipline was done I would gather Lass up in my big brown arms. I would caress her head, rub her chest and whisper in her ear, "It's all over, girl!"

Her eyes would shine again. Her whole frame would tremble with joy. There was total reconciliation, restoration. In pure pleasure she would leap out of my arms, race around on the grass in a wide circle and come leaping back into my warm embrace. It was her way of telling me how fond she was of me. "I'm all yours, Boss!"

Perhaps the most poignant and powerful memory that lingers with me about this delightful dog was her increasing willingness to do anything I asked of her. She was totally, instantly available for any task, no matter how tough or trying.

On the ranch we had some rather rugged, rough cut-over country. The sheep would scatter out into this difficult terrain of rock outcrops, wild rose thickets, downed timber and windfalls. They were searching for special sweet mouthfuls of grass and leaves not grazed before.

Because of my height, or because of keeping

27

steady count on the sheep, I always knew or could see where the lambs and ewes were in the broken country. Lass could not. So I would have to send her into these tough spots to round up and bring out the entire flock. For her it was virtually "going in blind," trusting me implicitly.

"Bring them in, Lass, bring them in!" I would command her. "Don't leave a single stray behind!"

She would go bounding away, over the rocks, through the windfalls, into the rose thickets—no matter the cost to herself. Often when she finally came out with all the flock, her face would be scratched, her fur would be clogged with burs, her feet would be cut or torn. But she had obeyed, never mind the suffering endured to do the job.

Because of such devotion, because of such faithful service, because of such loving loyalty great bonds of mutual respect, trust and affection were built between us.

28   Looking back across those precious years at "Fairwinds" I was learning from Lass exactly what it was that Christ, my Great Shepherd, wanted to do with me in His fields as His coworker. More and more clearly I was learning simple lessons of tremendous worth.

LESSON 1

In the Wrong Hands

It was pointed out at the beginning of this book
that, as the owner of "Fairwinds," I quickly realized I would need help to run the ranch and handle
the flock efficiently. That assistance had to come
from a faithful, loyal border collie, bred and disci-
plined for this unique and important work.

Though I was an energetic young man with a
strong set of legs and excellent lungs I simply could
not round up the sheep alone. The flock often scattered and fled in five directions when I tried to
gather them up alone on foot. No matter how fast I
ran or how loud I shouted the sheep still strayed in
their own stubborn way.

So I was obliged to find a coworker, a helper—
an "under-shepherd," if you will—in a sheep dog

who would carry out my will and my wishes in managing my stock. Working together with each other in harmony, good will, and mutual delight, one good sheep dog and myself could accomplish as much as five men.

In a touching, moving way, the same precise principle holds true in God's dealing with the world of men and women. The Lord called Himself the Good Shepherd. He pictured Himself for us as the one who had come to care for the "lost sheep." He carefully instructed His disciples to be His co-laborers who were to feed and tend His ewes and lambs.

It will be recalled how, after His resurrection, Jesus met His young friends beside the Lake of Galilee, and there prepared them a breakfast of fresh baked fish and chappatis. When the meal was over He turned to the big, rough fisherman Peter, asking him three times:

"Peter, do you really love me? Are you really my friend?" When the burly young man assured the Master of his loyalty and love, Jesus responded three times by saying:

"Peter, feed my lambs."

"Peter, feed my sheep."

"Peter, feed my sheep."

In the Wrong Hands

This was the special labor, the unique work, the specific purpose to which he was assigned.

It has been well said that "God has no hands in the world but our hands. He has no feet here but our feet. He has no lips but our lips." This is but another way of stating the rather obvious case that in a mysterious yet wondrous way our Father God chooses to carry on His purpose upon the planet through the fallible agency of common people most of the time.

He can, and, on rare occasions, does break through into human affairs in supernatural ways. Yet in the main He chooses to use us ordinary people to accomplish His grand designs. Seen in this dimension we begin to perceive the enormous honor and divine dignity He bestows on those of us chosen to become His coworkers.

Very often, as in my first encounter with Lass, He finds us cast in the wrong role, caught in the toils of our own intransigence, abused and misused by the wrong hands of an uncaring master.

This truth struck me with tremendous impact the day I drove up to the lady's gate and heard her rant and rave about her "crazy collie." Obviously the two long years they had spent together had been torture. She had no inkling of how to handle such a beautiful creature, bred for such special service, capable of such great good.

Nor did she seem to care a whit that all the potential locked up in this animal had gone wrong.

It was a profound portrait of so many of us people. It almost moved me to tears. For in the dusty dog, crouched in the dirt, hobbled with chains, glaring cold defiance, I saw portrayed the plight of so many men and women who, originally destined for great and noble service, have fallen into the wrong hands. Now they groveled in the dust and despair of wasted, misspent years.

The skilled master-breeders of the border counties in Britain had produced sheep dogs of acute intelligence and enormous energy. Their border collies were capable of outstanding service. And a beautiful specimen like Lass carried within her the capacity for outstanding work.

But, and "but" is a very big word just here, she had to be in the right hands! She had to come into the care of a good shepherd. She had to have her old habits broken, her energies redirected, and her remarkable instincts channeled into the precise purposes for which she had been bred.

Precisely the same principle holds true for us people. We have been created in the generous sov-

34

ereignty of God to achieve great things with Him. He endows us with the inherent capacity to carry out His will and do His work in the world, as we work together under His care. He is eager to see us share with Him in the sublime out-working of His purposes upon the planet. Together it is His intention that we should touch many lives, enrich many spirits and bring many souls into His special care and management.

For this to happen we must be loosed from the tyranny of the wrong owner. We must be released from servitude to sin, to self, to our sinister slavemaster, Satan.

This implies, of course, that a person is unshackled from one owner, to be brought under the management of another. There is no such thing as "absolute freedom." For even though human beings are free agents, by the very virtue of the facts of life, they must of necessity come under the control of forces and influences greater than themselves.

35

Often, young people especially boast of being "free" to do as they wish, to go wherever they will, or become whatever they choose. This is only partially true. For in actual fact, though they may not always realize it, their decisions, their behavior, their life style are not those of their own free will. Rather, they are conditioned, shaped and directed by the hands that govern them.

The word "hand" or "hands," used in a spiritual sense and divine dimension, refers to the influences of good or evil which play upon our lives. They are those forces of either the selfless love of a compassionate God, or the sinister selfishness of destructive demonic power at work in the world.

Unfortunately, Lass had fallen into the wrong hands. Under the misdirection and mishandling of the wrong owner, all her talent had been twisted and subverted for destructive ends. Her vigor, her vitality, her energy, her instincts were being wasted unduly on chasing boys and bicycles. Her capacity for fine worthwhile work was expended on the empty pursuit of cars.

The upshot was, bit by bit, link by link, day by day, she herself unwittingly, unknowingly was actually forging the shackles of steel that bound her to the ground.

We do exactly the same. Jesus Himself stated very categorically: "Every one who commits sin is a slave to sin" (John 8:34, RSV).

Those who often brag about being so very free, of "doing their own thing," of "flinging off all restraints," seldom realize they are inexorably bound and shackled by their own destructive life style. They are tethered by their own tyranny. They are trapped in the toils of their own destructive decisions and desires.

Nor can they be set free, unshackled, loosed except by the loving, caring, understanding hands of the Good Shepherd.

As I approached Lass on that momentous day that I found her in such a forlorn state, she met me with blazing eyes, low growls and bared teeth. She did not even want me to touch her. She did not want me to lay my hand upon her head. She trembled at the tone of my unfamiliar voice.

This was not surprising.

She had been so misused, so abused, so twisted and torn in spirit.

How or why should she trust anyone else?

And this is precisely the same with so many of us when first the Great Shepherd, the Christ of Galilee comes to us by His Spirit with outstretched hands of love, peace and understanding. We resist His very approach. We resent His voice calling to us. We recoil in fear and apprehension from His overtures of good will.

Deep within us doubts and misgivings surge

37

through our minds and emotions. Our spirits shrivel up within us. We cringe from His coming. We feel so threatened. Our wills are set in stern resistance. We are convinced we will only suffer more abuse at His hands.

But it is only the hand of God that sets us free.

It is His strong hands that can turn us around and train us to move in new ways, new directions.

It is His gentle, yet strong hands, His understanding hands, which can handle us with skill and love and strength.

It is His hands which can change our character, alter our conduct and send us out to do great and noble service in society.

The first owner Lass had did not understand dogs. She did not care about the lofty capabilities of this beautiful creature. She wanted only to get rid of Lass as quickly as possible.

Few of us, who have not yet come into Christ's care, think seriously enough about the sinister and subversive character of Satan. In fact, to many people he is almost less than real. He is sometimes supposed to be nothing more than a superstitious phantom, more or less the mere product of man's imagination.

The terrible truth is he is very real, very active

38

and exceedingly deceptive. While appearing to give us liberty by allowing us to do whatever we wish in response to our own inherent selfishness or sin, he watches us actually enslave and destroy ourselves.

Ultimately, as in the case of Lass, unless a new owner had intervened, she would have been destroyed. There really was no other alternative!

Happily that did not happen to her. A stranger showed up in her back yard that day. His coming would change the entire tenor of her life. This one who came looked with longing and love into those beautiful brown eyes of hers so filled with mingled hate and fear. He saw beyond the dirt and dust that clogged her mottled coat. He saw the magnificent head, the strong constitution, the beautiful body so well proportioned. He knew full well the powerful potential for good locked up within this tormented creature.

So bravely, boldly, without fear, I unshackled her chains and unhobbled her legs. I put my own soft collar upon her and took her away to my home.

She had passed from one set of hands into another set of hands. At first it was all terrifying. But one day she would know it was all very wonderful.

39

LESSONS FROM A SHEEP DOG

Many of us human beings have been under the wrong management most of our lives. We have been in the wrong hands. We have been so mishandled that all of the original, superb purposes for which we were created have been totally distorted and misspent. We are virtual slaves to sin, to ourselves and to Satan.

Yet the Stranger of Galilee comes into our lives. He looks upon us with love. He touches us with tenderness. He sees beyond our sins. He extends His knowing hands to take us into His understanding care.

We are not always keen to go.

We are afraid He may have sinister motives.

We recoil from His control.

Life under the old master has made us very suspicious. We are not at all sure things will be any better now.

In our human ignorance and suspicion we are convinced that to come into Christ's care can be even worse bondage than before.

As I put Lass into my old car and started off down the road to "Fairwinds" she was sure something terrible was about to happen. She crouched on the floor behind my seat, trembling and tense with apprehension. Even when I stretched out my hand to touch her head, or spoke to her softly in reassuring tones, she withdrew in terror, snarling with tension.

Little did that sad, twisted dog realize that one day soon she would enjoy those same hands and respond to that voice with unabashed devotion. But it would take time. It would take weeks and months for her to fully discover that her new master had only her best interests at heart. That every move he made was for her well-being.

It takes some of us a lifetime to learn that Christ, our Good Shepherd, knows exactly what He is doing with us. He understands us perfectly. He manages us with incredible wisdom and loving skill both for our benefit and His.

Bless His Name!

LESSON 2

Set Free — to Follow

Long before the day came that I brought Lass home to stay with us, I had painstakingly prepared a brand new kennel for the special dog that would share our life at "Fairwinds." In my mind's eye I had pictured a beautiful border collie that would work with me on the ranch, share in all the care of the sheep, and thus become a virtual member of our family.

There was a new leash as well; there were also sturdy, clean dishes to hold fresh food and clear cold water. Everything was in readiness for the particular dog chosen with great, loving care to be my companion and coworker. There was so much at stake in this selection. The successful operation of the ranch depended on a good dog. The skillful handling of the sheep was bound up in the creature's capacity to work obediently. My own joy and contentment in managing the flock rested in her responsiveness to my commands.

All of these hopes, dreams and aspirations moved through my mind as I drove home with Lass in the car. At last we pulled up at our gate. Gently I opened it, then we drove carefully over to our rustic cottage perched on a rise of ground overlooking the sea.

Here in our country setting all was tranquil. Only the wind in the trees, the tide running against the rocks, the gulls and crows wheeling and crying in the breeze above the shore, broke the silence.

There would be no boys racing by on bicycles. No cars roaring up the road. No traffic din or city noises to distract and disturb the dog. She was coming into a totally new setting of quiet serenity. She was entering the life of a brand-new master. What would she do?

46 Her initial reaction was to slink away, crouched low in the grass, in commingled fear and foreboding. Had she not been on a long leash she would have fled into the nearby forest that grew tall behind our home.

Speaking to her softly, petting her gently, trying to reassure her of my affection, I led her to the fine, new kennel standing in the shade of a lovely gnarled oak nearby. She simply stared at it, refusing to enter. Instead she stubbornly crouched at the entrance staring up at me with cold, hard, defiant eyes.

My wife, thrilled and excited by the beautiful dog, brought out a heaping bowl of fresh food for Lass. I fetched another dish full of cold, clear water for her. But she ignored both of our offerings. She refused to touch either the food or drink.

This went on day after day.

I was utterly dismayed.

There was no sign of positive response.

She began to lose condition. Her form became gaunt and wasted as day followed day.

So in a bold and daring act I undid her leash and set her totally free.

In a flash she was gone. Like a fleeing phantom she vanished into the woods. And I began to wonder if ever I would see her again.

For several days I drove up and down our country road in hope of finding her. I called at neighboring ranches. I combed our fields and ocean edge. But no sign of Lass.

In the anguish of my search, in the agony of my despair over her intransigence I began to understand a little of the sorrow and remorse God our

47

Father endures, amid all His endeavors to draw us into His family. Again and again we refuse all His benefits offered to us. Belligerently we often rebuff all His love and concern.

Yet, in spite of all her indifference, in spite of her reluctance to respond, in spite of her twisted, unyielding resistance and resentment I had an enormous empathy for the dog. In a profound way I longed to redeem her. I was consumed with a powerful desire to turn her around and make her into a loving, loyal companion. In a passionate way I yearned to see her rise to the potential that lay dormant within her.

All of these hopes seemed dashed into dust, until one evening I happened to look up onto the edge of a rough rock outcrop behind the cottage. There she was! Like a crouched cougar she stared down at me. There was still a chance that contact might be made between us.

48   I decided to take food and water up to her lookout. Every morning it was gone. And yet every evening she would be back. Every time I approached her, called her by name, or whistled, she vanished from view, spirited away like smoke whisked away in the wind.

Dark doubts began to intrude themselves into my mind and emotions. I began to wonder if in fact this distant dog would ever become truly mine. She did not mind eating the food set out for her; she drank the water poured out for her; she relished the total freedom she had been given.

But she was not mine. Nor was I hers!

Caught up in this stand-off, the gracious Spirit of God brought home to my heart with great clarity the peculiar predicament in which people put themselves before God.

The Master comes to us in our plight. He offers to take us into His family. He spares no pains to provide all that is necessary for our welfare and contentment in His care. He speaks to us reassuringly. He calls us by name. He sets us totally free.

Yet the personal, private response of most people is to recoil from Him. They resent His approach. They choose very deliberately to refuse to respond to His overtures of deep compassion. They flee to escape from His hands.

The peculiar, perverse paradox in all of this belligerent behavior is that at the same time they do not mind taking advantage of Christ's benefits, but at the moment and place of their own choosing in their own self-willed way.

This is being acted out every day in thousands of ways in human society. It is a prominent part of the social scene in so-called "Christian" circles. It is a tragic part of the picture in so much pastoral work.

In literally thousands of lives God in Christ has come and actually set people "free." He has placed before them all the benefits and delights of belonging to His family. He has made available to them His love, His care, His provisions in generous measure.

In spite of all this, their liberty and freedom is used only for selfish ends. They insist on "doing their own thing—in their own way—at their own time." They are not a particle of use to the Master. They are at a distance. They are not under His control. So all the good of which they are capable comes to nothing.

One night a few ewes and lambs grazed up near the rock where Lass would lay. I saw her sit up, cock her head and watch them with great intensity. Perhaps her latent instincts to shepherd sheep were coming to life.

So evening after evening when the day's chores were done, I would direct a few sheep toward her . . . hoping somehow this might help to establish rapport or contact between us.

But nothing seemed really to elicit her positive response. Week was now following week. I began to wonder very seriously if all my overtures of love were in vain. The dark prospect that she might have to be destroyed loomed ever larger.

This was a most poignant lesson I learned from this dog. It was she who eventually must make the decision whether or not she would come to me, entrust her life to my care, allow me to control her conduct.

At this point in my own personal walk with God I had been much bewildered by the conflicting views and highly divergent doctrines debated within Christendom. Discussions on the absolute sovereignty of God as held by the extreme Calvinists, and the grave responsibility of man as taught by the Arminians had always dismayed me. For in the final analysis the issue always arises as to the ultimate end of man.

Does he decide his own destiny?

Does he determine his own destruction?

Does he discover that "hell" or "heaven" are of his own choice, not God's?

In my agonizing approaches and appeals to Lass I saw with intense, spiritual clarity that both views were correct, both concepts were complementary, both views were totally reconciled within the response of an individual's will.

As her new master, I had done absolutely everything I could within my special power and sovereign love for her. Now she, in response to my compassionate care for her, would have to choose to come to me of her own free will, yet ever drawn by my overtures of concern.

The last thing in the world I wanted at this point was to have this dog destroyed. Just the thought grieved me. I cringed from the very prospect of losing this lovely creature.

God's Word is very clear, very specific in this whole matter. He does not come to condemn us. He does not desire to destroy us. He does not send us to destruction.

We ourselves choose what our end shall be.

We are free to follow our own feeble, foolish ways, or we are free to follow Him who came to deliver us from the despair of our own dilemma.

It was with such tremendous truths surging through my own spirit that I would go out at twilight to try and draw this irascible creature to myself. Steadily my hopes grew dimmer. The period of six weeks probation was almost run out. The crucial hour of final reckoning was just around the corner. My spirit would not always strive with Lass. Her prospects were fading.

Then one beautiful, summer evening the sun

52

was setting in a spectacle of golden glory over the western horizon. The mingled colors of rose, lavender, gold and scarlet were reflected in the sea. In the foreground my flock fed peacefully in the pastures at the ocean edge. It was utterly still, breathtaking—a scene which transported one into a sense of wondrous serenity.

Lass was not even foremost in my mind at the time.

But suddenly, softly, almost imperceptibly amid my reverie I sensed the pensive, hesitant, first faint touch of a warm, soft nose touching my hands held behind my back.

An electric excitement shot through me.

A thrill of exquisite delight swept over me.

Lass had come! Contact had been made! The distance between us had been crossed!

It was a heart-stopping moment.

Joy, irrepressible joy, swept through me in wave upon wave.

Hope flamed anew!

All would be well!

Fully, completely, clearly I could see now why Christ told us emphatically there was tremendous joy in heaven whenever a straying one came home. I could understand why all the pent-up hopes, desires and dreams of God for His people, when brought to reality, set the angels singing. I could grasp in a singular way why it is that in a single soul's response to God's love, there is reason for celestial celebration.

Without, in any way, being either presumptuous or even sacrilegious, I felt I had stood where Christ stands, and felt as He feels, in that rapt moment when a wanderer comes to Him at last.

Lass discovered, to her delight, that what she had found was not new chains, or abuse or bondage. What she had come home to was warmth, understanding, affection, and the thrilling freedom to fulfill the purposes for which she had been bred.

All she had to do was to follow me!

It was I who would introduce her for the first time into a remarkable relationship of mutual trust, of undivided loyalty, of happy comradeship, of joyous adventures, of worthwhile work she had never experienced before.

As I stroked her beautiful head, ran my hands over her deep wide chest, spoke to her reassuringly in soft, tender tones, she knew at last she was where she truly belonged.

54

She had finally found courage to put herself in the master's hands. And in this choice she had found unlimited liberty for the rest of her life—the liberty of being a loving friend and servant.

It was a touching interlude that evening. It was a glorious moment in my life, never to be forgotten. In the fading twilight she followed me home to the cottage, quietly entered her kennel, and lay down to rest in peace and contentment.

The lesson is so clear, so powerful, so profound it needs no further elaboration here. The choice is ours whether or not we will come to Christ our Good Shepherd. The decision is ours whether or not we will decide to follow Him.

For the person who does, it is to discover His boundless love, His enormous good will, His generous care, His wondrous knowing management of their lives, His affectionate acceptance into His family.

In all of this there lies liberty, contentment and total fulfillment.

LESSON 3

Learning to Trust

For the first few weeks of our intimate acquaint-
ance, Lass was like a highly strung musical
instrument. The lightest touch of my hands upon
her made the high-strung creature tremble with
tension. So long had she been out of tune with life
that it took the new master's knowing hands a con-
siderable time to bring her into harmony with
himself.

If I touched her unexpectedly she would tend to
recoil, tense herself in readiness to run, then stand
trembling, not quite sure of my intentions. In her
subconscious mind lingered the dark shadows of
the abuse she had suffered before in the wrong
hands.

Little by little, day upon day, time after time I

would take her into my arms just to hold her close. At first she could endure this only for a few moments. Then with a sudden leap she would bound out of my embrace, wondering if I really meant well. The old fears of former years still haunted her.

But when I brushed her thick, lustrous, shining coat it seemed to set her apprehension at ease. When I carefully removed the burs from her body she knew and sensed with her acute intelligence that I truly cared about her condition. She even learned to let me pull the angry wild rose thorns from between her toes. She sometimes tried in vain to draw them out with her teeth. So when I took them out, and the burning ceased, she would lick my hands in gratitude.

In all of these intimate, personal contacts I began to discern clearly that I was as much her servant as she was mine. God's gentle Spirit showed me in living, vivid reality the enormous condescension of Christ, my Master, who in love and self-humiliation tends my human needs.

The lesson I was beginning to learn slowly is that God, very God, does indeed become our love-slave. He comes to comfort. He comes to heal. He comes to help. He comes to be our ministering companion—our alongside comrade.

60

In reciprocation of affection, in genuine gratitude for His generosity, in profound appreciation
for His tender touch upon my life, there is born
within me the desire to be His love-slave. Or to put
it in the simple words of Scripture, "We love him,
because he first loved us!" (1 John 4:19).

This basic interchange of loving concern and
real care for each other was the bedrock upon
which trust and confidence was built between this
beautiful dog and myself. Steadily she was learning what it meant to be set free into a new dimension of dynamic devotion to her new owner. She
was discovering the stimulus of being useful, of
being a benefit, of being essential in the master's
service.

Too many of us have the wrong view of work
with God. Too many of us look upon it more or less
as a grim bondage. Too many of us regard it as a
sort of serfdom. No, no, no! For when we truly
come to know His touch upon our lives, and sense
the sweetness of His Spirit at work in our souls, we
are aware of being liberated into joyous experiences and adventurous undertakings of enormous
enthusiasm.

For Lass, a part of this wondrous new world of
hers was the sound of my voice. With the passing
weeks she learned to listen for it. She came to

understand its timbre and tone. She discovered that I meant what I said.

Unlike her former owner who ranted and raved, screamed and threatened in angry tirades, there was none of that.

When I called her she quickly discovered that she was fully expected to come. She would be petted and praised. She would be shown that her compliance and cooperation were mutually delightful.

To hear my voice was to alert herself to respond to it. For as week followed week she rapidly realized I was not one to waste words, indulge in empty emotions, or give false commands.

What I said I meant.

What I told her she could trust.

What I commanded she was expected to carry out.

This did not happen in a day. It did not take place in a week. It was a steady, ongoing process in which she came to respect and respond to my voice.

When I spoke she would cock her ears to catch every syllable. She would tilt her head to one side a little, listening with intense concentration. She would fasten her shining eyes upon my face—alert, eager, ready to move into immediate action.

There was something very stimulating in such

62

behavior. In this powerful response to the sound of my voice, I saw trust and faith and confidence grow between us.

Most important, what I learned from Lass is how faith, likewise, grows between me and God—how quiet confidence comes into play between me and my Master, Jesus Christ—how acute sensitivity is established between me and the Gracious Spirit.

For God does speak. God has articulated Himself. His voice has gone out through all the earth. He speaks through His own written Word. He speaks through His prophets of old. He speaks through Christ. He speaks through His own people today. He speaks through His own Spirit within us. He speaks through the wonder of His own created universe.

Like Lass, do I alert myself to hear His voice? Do I set myself to be sensitive to His sounds? Do I truly concentrate on His commands? Am I ready to respond with alacrity to His wishes?

Faith comes by "hearing" in this way. And hearing comes by and through the Word of God to us (Romans 10:17).

And the lifetime lesson learned from working with Lass was simply this: *"Faith is my personal, positive response to the Word of God, to the point where I act in quiet trust."*

63

LESSONS FROM A SHEEP DOG

This Lass was learning to do with me. This she was finding out was actually "fun" for both of us. It was the secret to success in our great adventures together on the ranch.

Bit by bit it was becoming clear to this dog that even when I corrected her, it was not with any ill will, but only for her good and mine. Not only was she beginning to understand that "I meant what I said," but also, "I said what I meant."

In short she saw that I was consistent in my commands. She trusted me more and more to act with integrity. She learned that she could rely on me to come through.

For me as her new master and her, as a dog in training, the excitement in seeing her twisted old traits being straightened out was a stimulating, happy interlude.

Lass was moving out into a whole new world of fresh and exciting encounters. She had never before been set free into such open fields where the wind moved over the grass in flowing motion. That same wind brought to her keen nostrils the strong stimuli of new sensations.

She was finding out all about sheep, about ewes and rams, and the frisky, gamboling lambs. She was coming across the pungent, powerful spoor of deer, raccoons, cougars and otters. She was watching the gulls and geese and wild brant winging above the waves. She was seeing the splash and spray of the sea bursting against the rocky shore.

There was life, energy, thrust and the pull of the natural world all around her. She was no longer a tiny pup learning from her mother the wisdom and ways of the wild. She had to learn now from me. She had to trust me to teach her all about the ranch and woods and life by the shining sea.

Amid all the new surroundings of forests and fields her latent instincts so far astray in town were steadily being brought into harmony with the natural world around her. It was a thrilling thing to see and sense how she literally "blossomed" in her behavior. She was finding the role in life for which she had been bred. She was growing into the joyous gaiety of living as she was always intended to live, guided by my continual presence.

Lass gave me the distinct impression that we were becoming the very best of friends. Insofar as it is possible for a dog to convey to its master the delight and pleasure it experiences, she let me know again and again that ranch life was a great game she enjoyed to the full.

65

But the best part, it seemed, was just being with me.

Now this is no small honor.

For it places upon the one so trusted great responsibility. Her happiness was literally in my hands. Her contentment was in my company. Her trust was in my integrity.

Where before she had at first shied away from me, now by degrees she became my very "shadow."

Strangers, friends, and visitors who came to "Fairwinds" often remarked about her single-minded devotion to me. They were amazed by her loyalty. They commented again and again: "She's your shadow."

Where I stood, she would come and stand.

Where I sat, she would come and sit beside me.

Where I walked, she would follow at my side.

We became inseparable companions.

All of this began to make an indelible impression upon my own spirit. Searching, stabbing questions came to me as to my own walk with my Master.

Was I this conscious of Christ?

Did I find life with Him an adventure?

Had I become so fond of His friendship that it surpassed all other interests?

66

Learning to Trust

Was the devotion I received from this beautiful dog any measure of my loyalty to my Master?

In utter honesty and devastating truth I had to admit my devotion fell far short of hers. Nor would it even begin to approach her level of trust for years yet to come.

Over and beyond all this Lass became what we sometimes refer to as "a one-man dog." She would eat only if I fed her. She would drink only the fresh water I set before her. She would permit only me to fondle and pet her intensively.

If it was necessary for me to be away, she would literally go on a fast until my return. She was unwilling to accept or partake of anything offered to her by others—not even my wife.

This single-minded fixation was an integral part of her personality. It was a measure of her character. It governed her conduct. Above all it was the hard core of our splendid success as coworkers on the ranch.

For it was based on this unwavering fidelity that I in turn could begin to trust her. I knew I could count on her "to come through." I could be sure that here was a sheep dog capable of great service as we learned to work together. The entire future of "Fairwinds" and the total welfare of the flock

67

under my care would in large measure hinge and turn upon our mutual trust . . . love . . . and loyalty.

This is why Jesus asked Peter again and again beside the lake, "Friend, do you really love Me? Are you really loyal? Do you truly trust Me?" Then, and only then could the rough-hewn fisherman be entrusted to tend the Master's flock.

And if we are serious in our desires to serve the Living Christ, the Great Good Shepherd, we must examine carefully our relationship to Him.

Can it be said of me, "He is a one-man person"? Is my dedication and devotion single-minded, centered and concentrated upon Christ?

From whose hand do I eat and drink?

Where do I get my nourishment and refreshment?

Am I willing to feed on the fare dished out to me by a wide diversity of worldly wiselings? Where do I turn for my mental, moral and spiritual stamina? What range of resources do I draw upon for refreshment and enthusiasm? Am I willing to be "watered" by anyone or anything that comes along appearing to be titillating to the senses? Am I easily satisfied by a sensual society?

It was from Lass that I learned the sterling les-

68

son that God can only truly trust those who truly trust Him. He gives Himself in wondrous plenitude to the person whose single-minded devotion, love and loyalty is given to the Lord.

And because of this mutual trust, those all around are enriched and blessed beyond their wildest imagination.

LESSON 4

The Delight of Obedience

As month followed month, the summer season giv-
ing way to the lovely autumn days, Lass and I were
caught up in great adventures together. Handling
the sheep, running the ranch, guarding against
possible predators were more than mere "work."
Rather, our life on the land was a great and joyous
pleasure. I say this in utter sincerity because this
beautiful border collie brought sparkling joy and
pleasure into my days.

It was from her that I learned the profound
lesson of what it really means "to please the Master"—"to bless God"—"to enrich the Spirit."

Lass was not a noisy dog. In fact, she was quite
quiet. She seldom barked except to warn of a
stranger's approach. When we worked together

she was almost totally silent. She did not yap needlessly. Her main energies were given to carrying out my commands. This was not always as easy as it sounds for she was no longer a young pup. A mature dog, already somewhat set in her ways, she had to learn to obey.

The lessons taught her were intense, clear, simple and uncomplicated. The words of command were sharp, short and to the point: *Come, Sit, Fetch, Stay, Stop, Down, Right, Left,* and so on. They were spoken clearly, explicitly, without waste of syllables.

By degrees she learned the precise meaning of each. Steadily she began to respond with alacrity and joy. Every correct move she made was rewarded with lavish praise and a hug of hearty approval. To obey was not a bore for her. It was happy cooperation with me. It was to carry out my will and wish with bright joy. She was swift to respond.

74 Strangers began to hear about this remarkable dog. Some would drive all the way out from the city, twenty-seven miles away, just to watch her work with me. They would stand pensively at the gate, asking permission to see how beautifully she obeyed my commands.

The Delight of Obedience

Again and again the most common comments they made were, "But she just loves to work with you! She enjoys carrying out your wishes! More than anything else she finds enormous pleasure in pleasing you by her obedience."

And this was true.

Not only was her faithful obedience a joy to me, but also a delight to her and an inspiration to onlookers.

In our quiet, happy hours together at "Fairwinds," as we went about our tasks together, there was ample time to reflect on this great lesson learned from Lass.

It became obvious to me that just as my will and wishes for this devoted dog were expressed in clear, concise terms, so likewise God's good will for me has been stated in simple, straightforward language in His Word.

God has not left us without clear instructions. His desires for us have been articulated in unmistakable terms. His Word is sharp, precise, to the point. And it is our humble responsibility to learn to respond to it with alacrity.

There is ever abroad among Christ's followers the element of confusion in which people claim not to know or understand clearly what His intentions are. There really is no excuse for this. Any person who truly desires to know and do God's good will can find it stated clearly in His Word to them.

The basic difficulty is not a lack of comprehension on our part. The question is simply the intransigence of our own tough, unyielded wills. Most of us will not submit to the control of Christ. We will not come under the good government of God. We will not respond to the sovereignty of His Spirit when He speaks to us.

The greatest delusion any man or woman can ever come under is the idea that it is a "drag" to do God's will. Just the opposite is true! Yet our old natures, our strong, selfish self-interests, our sensual society, our arch-foe Satan—all endeavor to deceive us into believing that it is a bore and bondage to serve the Master, to carry out His commands in glad-hearted cooperation.

Part of this is associated with the tired, traditional old idea of serving God "in fear." The use of this word "fear" all through the Old Testament scriptures, has, most unfortunately, left the wrong impression upon our minds. And it was Lass, more than anyone else, who brought me to a clear concept of its true meaning.

"To fear," with regard to God, means to rever-

76

ence, to respect, to regard with awe and affection, to hold in such loving esteem as to be afraid of offending or grieving the One so admired.

This was the attitude Lass held toward me. It had been built on trust. It had grown gradually with the realization she could count on the consistency of my conduct and the credibility of my character. She had come to see me as more than just her master, but also her friend. We were fellow-workers in the great responsibilities of running the ranch. Her loyalty was grounded in love.

This is precisely what Jesus, our Lord, referred to when He spoke so intimately to His eleven disciples just before His death: "Ye are my friends, if ye do whatsoever I command you. Henceforth I call you not servants; for the servant knoweth not what his lord doeth: But I have called you friends" (John 15:14–15).

Ultimately, finally, our love for God is demonstrated not by some soft, sentimental emotion, but rather in implicit obedience to His will, expressed in our loving cooperation with His commands.

When we comply with His wishes in happy cooperation, our walk with Him, our work with Him, our way with Him become a deep delight. Not only is He immensely pleased, but so also are we.

77

LESSONS FROM A SHEEP DOG

It never ceased to amaze and stimulate me to see how thrilled Lass was in her whole-hearted obedience. Her eyes would literally sparkle, shine and snap with pure pleasure. Her tail would wag with joy. Her beautiful body was electric, charged, vibrant with ecstatic satisfaction.

This is what she had been designed to do.

This is what her breed had been developed to achieve.

·This was the purpose for which she was placed upon the planet.

And precisely the same held true for me in my personal relationship with Christ. The question was, did I realize this?

Most of us do not!

I did not come into this interaction with God until I was a man well into my forties. It takes some of us "old dogs" much longer to learn new tricks than it ever took Lass to learn to love and obey me.

Oh, how tough, stubborn and stupid are some of our souls.

I confess here with burning shame and bowed head that though this dear dog was a living, vibrant example of what it means to be obedient, my strong will was slow, slow, slow to learn this same lesson.

The Delight of Obedience

It would be at least ten more years before I could declare fearlessly with the psalmist of old:

"I delight to do thy will, oh my God:
Yea, thy law (word) is within my heart (my will)"

(Psalm 40:8).

Lass had a lot to unlearn.
But she was eager and anxious to obey.
At heart what she wanted was my approval.
This is a point that escapes many of us. We seem rather casual and quite indifferent to whether or not our conduct does meet with the Master's approval. Do we really care what He thinks of our character? A sobering question!
As the gentle, blue haze of Indian summer days settled softly over our coastline the whole world seemed wrapped in wonder. Long wavering skeins of Canada geese and black brant were silhouetted against the sky. Flocks of sea birds settled in our sheltered bays. Great flights of band-tailed pigeons came to gorge on the ripening acorns in the giant oaks. The acorns they knocked to the ground were a special delicacy for the sheep now becoming fat and fit for the winter weather.

LESSONS FROM A SHEEP DOG

Lass, like me, had come to love "Fairwinds." She reveled in all the sights and smells and sounds of the natural world pulsing around us. Each new dawn was the beginning of a bright new adventure. She was keen to go, eager to live, ready to learn any fresh new lesson.

Of these by far the most advanced and demanding were working to hand signals, instead of spoken words of command. By combining the two together at first she gradually, surely made the transition from one to the other.

For instance, if she was running toward me at high speed, I only had to raise my arm vertically, with hand fully extended, and she would drop to the ground at once. This was the signal for *"Stop"!*

It was essential that she master this means of communication. First, because I was often at great distances from her, almost out of voice range. So it saved shouting and yelling. Secondly, it was much less disturbing to the sheep, and to the tranquil scenes in which we worked together, if we communicated in comparative silence and quiet mutual understanding.

For this sort of command to work well between us, Lass had to learn to keep me in view and give me her constant, undivided attention.

The parallel relationship in our own walk and

work with our Master is most important. For as we mature in our spiritual lives we come to understand clearly the providential "hand" of God guiding us.

Early in our experiences with Christ it is imperative always that we discover and determine His will for us in and through the "Word spoken." In time, and with constant application, this word grows so familiar, so well established, so much a force within our wills that it becomes natural and normal for us to comply with His commands.

We then move on to the position where we sense and detect His will being expressed to us by the providential handling of our lives. We actually begin "to look for God's hand" in all the details and events of our days. We become acutely sensitive to His presence. We find our minds, spirits and emotions concentrated on Christ, eager to do His bidding.

This does not happen overnight. Nor does it take place in one short burst of devotion. As with the long months it took Lass to learn hand commands, so it takes us years, in some cases, to sense the unmistakable hand of God active in our affairs, leading us surely, directing us in every detail of our personal pilgrimage.

For me as a man this has, without any question,

become the most thrilling aspect of life with the Master—the constant awareness of His presence, the action of His hand directing in the minutiæ of the moment, His arrangement of events with precision, His sure guidance in stillness and serenity.

I know of no greater "good," no more exalted "joy" than this quiet, harmonious, pleasant partnership. As I understand it, this is what it means to be "a friend of God."

It far surpasses and transcends all the fanfare and hyper razzle-dazzle that makes up so much of modern religious activity.

It is God and His coworker quietly getting God's work done in the world. That counts most in eternal values.

This means, therefore, that the communion between Christ and me is very intimate, harmonious and complementary. We are not at odds. There is no strain or tension between us, but rather a superb rapport.

82

A special point, which simply must be emphasized here, is that the end result of the remarkable collaboration between Lass and myself was the enormous benefit that also came to both the sheep and the whole ranch because of her beautiful behavior. Through her prompt, explicit obedience the sheep were moved easily, not harassed unduly. They were handled through her swift, smooth actions with a minimum of disturbance and distraction.

Just as Lass learned to love, respect and respond to me, so the sheep soon discovered that Lass meant them no harm, but was only carrying out commands intended for their best interests. They learned they could not outwit her, outrun her or outflank her. Their contentment in turn was to do what she wanted them to do, because that really was "the Master's wishes."

The whole ranch flourished and prospered as Lass and I were increasingly integrated into a smoothly functioning team. Everything turned on our joyous cooperation and hearty compatibility.

Precisely the same holds true for us in our contacts with those other lives that God entrusts us to touch. If men and women are ever going to see and understand something of the generous good will of God it has to be through our implicit obedience and joyous devotion to Him. If they are to grasp the unique and special sterling character of Christ who cares for them it must be through our personal fondness and reflection of Him as our "friend."

As I saw with Lass, this is how the Master truly

intends His work to be done in this dreary old world. His work can be done with delight and it can be done so beautifully that others will benefit beneath the guidance of His great, good hand.

LESSON 5

The Test of Faithfulness

During our working years together, several little problem areas began to appear in the dog's behavior. In that strange way so common to all of us, one of her greatest strengths also became the point of her greatest weakness.

It was the whole matter of wanting to keep me in view at all times. Lass had a passionate fixation on being with me, near me, and in action beside me. This intense loyalty contributed enormously to her own prompt and happy obedience. It was what enabled her to react to my hand signals so well.

So it can be understood why the one command which she found most difficult to carry out was "Stay." This brief, strong, explicit word meant for her to remain steady wherever she was placed.

LESSONS FROM A SHEEP DOG

On a sheep ranch, part of the success with sheep involves moving them continuously from pasture to pasture. It also means intensive management of the flock from time to time in sorting out ewes, lambs and rams. Only with the eager assistance of a good sheep dog can these operations be carried out smoothly, efficiently and without undue disturbance for the sheep or owner.

At such times it meant I might ask her to "Stay" and guard an open gate. Or she might be expected to hold a small band of ewes in a corner while I checked their lambs. Or it might be any one of a dozen other little tasks that demanded her to be steadfast, alert, quietly on guard while I was busy about other duties.

Somehow Lass often felt she was missing out on the action in these situations. If I disappeared from her view she was sure she had been forgotten. She would become very uneasy, begin to move about, then "break faith" or "break trust" to take off in search of me.

When I came back to find her gone, it was always a severe disappointment. The sheep would quickly scatter, our work would be undone, and the task would have to be started all over again.

Lass, of course, could not always fully com-

prehend the complexity of the work we were doing.
And at times she gave me the distinct impression
that for a dog as eager and energetic as she was, to
"stay" was almost asking too much of her.

Because I, too, am an individual of great drive,
endued with energy and enthusiasm, God used
this element in Lass to teach me a most important
principle. I began to grasp the absolute necessity
to be quietly steadfast and faithful wherever He
placed me. In a sense these quiet interludes in life
were a superb test not only of my faithfulness to
God, but also of His to me.

Such times of "stillness," of apparent "inac-
tion," as may come to any of us are not necessarily
a trial for the lethargic or easygoing individual.
But for the person eager to be in the thick of
things, who wants to see action, who is keen for
visible, vibrant evidence of the Master at work,
these are tough and testing times. We seem to be in
a stale situation. It may even appear to us as a
waste of time. We may feel we are forgotten by
God, passed up or overlooked in His program. To
use a rather colloquial phrase, we think we are
"on the shelf."

In fact, looking back in retrospect now, I realize with acute humiliation that even during those

89

years at "Fairwinds" I sometimes felt that way toward Christ. I often wondered why I should be "stuck" with this flock of sheep. I wondered why the Lord did not allow me to get into greater action in other areas of life. It was hard to see then that a supreme lesson I was learning was to be steadfast just where He put me.

At such times we do not have the "greater view" of the great, good Shepherd. We do not always see His hand at work. We seem to be caught up in silence with no new clear commands coming to us. We are sorely tempted "to break faith"; to take the initiative into our own wills; to make the next move all on our own.

It has often been said that almost any of us can be heroic, dashing, even daring in the midst of great excitement. But it takes a much more steadfast, quiet, strong faith in our Father to "stay true" in the quiet place where He puts us. It is in the daily, drab, often humdrum duties of our little lives where God asks us to be loyal, steady friends—people who will perform their part without fanfare or flamboyancy, those who can be trusted implicitly to do their duty.

In reflecting back on those days with Lass I am still stirred by the memories of the times when she proved so true to me. I can recall vividly how

90

thrilled I was to come back and find she had stuck to her post and played her part well. How I would pat and praise her! And how she reveled in my adulation!

It is exactly the same for us. Christ will again make His presence very apparent to us. He need not be grieved or disappointed. He can be given the great joy of finding us faithful in the place He puts us.

His measurement of our success does not always lie in our spectacular activities. Sometimes it lies in our quiet steadfastness for Him. He does not always expect us to fully understand all His management of our lives. But He does ask us to stay true to Him today.

It was at this point in her total performance that Lass was often exposed to the most severe temptations. Of these by far the most tormenting, for a greater part of the year, was a flock of crows that nested on a nearby island.

The noisy, black rascals had chosen to establish a regular rookery in the gnarled, wind-twisted trees that clung to the rock outcrop offshore. There in the thick, wind-tossed tangle of tough branches they built their nests, laid their eggs and reared their fledglings.

LESSONS FROM A SHEEP DOG

Because of the rocky shoreline, the swift running tides and often stormy sea, they felt safe and secure from molestation by either man or natural predators. The result was that scores of crows were constantly flying back and forth from the little island, across our meadows, in search of food for their young.

In the usual manner of these crafty birds, they were alert to any danger. They regarded Lass and me as intruders in their territory, and seemed to find some fiendish pleasure in tormenting us with their raucous cries and spectacular, daring dives.

For the dog, especially, they became a formidable temptation in distracting her from her duties. The big, noisy birds would come streaming out of their trees to swoop low over Lass with jeering "caws" and tormenting tactics. They would skim down just above her head, the wind whistling through their wing tips, like dive bombers swooping to the attack.

The distraction was so strong that again and again Lass's will would break and she would tear away after them, leaping, barking, racing over the fields in wild abandon. Of all the dogs I have owned across the years, Lass was, without doubt, one of the swiftest. Her well-formed, strongly mus-

cled frame seemed almost to float above the fields
as she swept after the crows in full flight.

It really was all great fun. At times I had the
clear impression that the crows engaged in this
game with a devilish glee. And when it was all over
Lass would come back spent and exhausted, her
tongue hanging out with weariness.

In one sense it all seemed very hilarious and
amusing. In fact she would look up into my face,
her head cocked to one side, as much as to say,
"What great sport that was! I really put them to
flight."

Actually in another dimension it was a serious
obstacle to the efficient operation of the ranch.
For what the crows did was to distract the dog from
her paramount duties. Their silly games sometimes wore her out and exhausted her energies for
useful service. Perhaps the most disagreeable part
was that the mischievous birds sometimes caused
Lass to break faith and tear off after them when
she was supposed to "Stay."

I often thought about the crows and how they
managed to intrude themselves into my management of the ranch. They flew in from outside the
property. They were in no way a part of it. Yet
their repeated appearances every spring, when

they returned from their winter migration to the south, were an alarming signal that we had to put up with their nuisance behavior all through the summer, until fall.

More than one of the more offensive birds fell to my gun, especially when they began to raid the garden. Yet I had much more important work to do than shoot crows.

In the contest with the belligerent birds I saw clearly a parallel that we people face in our service for God. There is no intention to enlarge on the subject here, except to say that often we are distracted from the Master's highest intentions for us by extenuating events in our lives.

Either people or circumstances which often have their origin outside the family of God, and are no part of His purposes for us, intrude themselves into our experience. On the surface, and at first appearance, they may seem harmless, exciting, even somewhat entertaining or amusing.

94

The difficulty is they distract us from our main and most important responsibilities to Christ. They call us away and tempt us to take off in hot pursuit. In the process our energies are wasted, our strength is expended—yet really the benefit either to God or His flock is nil.

It may all appear as a very spectacular show. It might even seem to us a legitimate and essential part of our service. Still, in the end, it really is not anything more than a "show," a "display," a "diversion." We fall prey to such performances almost unwittingly and unknowingly.

Without being unduly critical or censorious, it is essential for each of us to examine our lives and ascertain what it is that diverts us from the highest duties to which God calls us as His co-workers. Within the community of our modern-day churches it is often the temptation to entertain rather than to edify God's people. It is the desire to amuse audiences rather than instruct them in God's Word. It is the tendency to titillate hearers rather than teach them life-changing truths. It is to become engrossed and carried away by that which the world considers glamorous rather than being centered and concerned in Christlike conduct and character.

The temptations come in many guises. But like the crows, though they were all shining in their bright plumage, they were black rascals bent on mischief.

It seemed a strange, fascinating irony at "Fair-winds" that in the autumn, about the time the crows flocked up for their fall migration to the sunny south, we began our land-clearing operations. With the summer work over, and the arrival of the gentle autumn rains, it was time to start tearing out underbrush, stumps and unwanted trees to provide new pastures for the ever-increasing flock of sheep.

Instead of crows to chase, Lass now turned her attention to the blazing sparks and flaming firebrands that would be carried up into the wind from the roaring fires. As the glowing cinders drifted across the gray, overcast skies she would go racing and leaping after them, barking furiously.

Often in the midst of my work I would have to stop and just watch the remarkable performance she put on. She would literally leap into midair snapping excitedly at the burning fragments borne aloft on the rising heat waves. Occasionally sparks would settle into her soft, silken, shining coat. There they would begin to smoulder, burn, then char her hair. It gave off a repulsive stench that drifted with the cool winter winds.

In further excitement ,Lass would roll in the damp grass, race around in the rain and snap furiously at the offending sparks that had set her afire. It was all very spectacular, but in reality it

96

did not help the work on the ranch one bit. It was of no use to the sheep or me. Most important, it wore her out completely. And during those times of testing when she was expected to stay steadfast caring for the sheep, it often took a single spark or two to undo all of our work, as well as our carefully prepared plans.

Of course these episodes in which Lass "let me down" came as a keen disappointment. Somehow she sensed that she had not been faithful. Our own land-clearing fires had been her undoing.

The same principle holds true within the church, within any community of Christians, but perhaps most importantly within our own private relationship to Christ Himself.

There is the ever-present tendency to be taken up with that which is highly emotional. People are always fascinated by excitement and ecstasy in any form. The long historical record of God's dealings with His people is shot through with instances where "false fire" and "strange sacrifices" led to disaster and disillusionment. Often it has its origin within the church itself. That which was intended by God to serve His own greater purposes for good becomes a diversion to us that undoes and nullifies our usefulness.

97

LESSONS FROM A SHEEP DOG

As many of God's great saints have stated so often, "The apparent good becomes the very thing which deprives us of God's best!"

Our loyalty is lost in lust.

It is worthy of our special consideration today that in society many of the most flamboyant "believers" often lack credibility. In their flaming zeal and inordinate preoccupation with dramatic displays there often is intermingled irresponsible sensuality that leads them astray.

There is a modern tendency in the church to be carried away with peripheral issues that take God's servants off on tangents. Too often the emphasis is on the dramatic rather than on the divine will and wishes of our God.

In working with Lass this lesson came home to me again and again. It is not the spectacular nor the sensational for which the Master looks. He seeks, instead, for me to simply be faithful wherever He places me in His all-wise plans and purposes.

LESSON 6

Love and Discipline

It will be obvious to the reader by now that the mutual love and affection which had been established between Lass and myself was very precious to both of us. It seemed to me at times that our intimate relationship was much more than merely a man and dog, more than a shepherd and his sheep dog, more even than efficient coworkers.

We had become special friends!

With her keen perception, sensitive instincts and acute intelligence, Lass had a special capacity not only to understand my commands but even more importantly to anticipate my wishes. It was this unusual awareness that made her such a remarkable worker.

In time she came to be worth two or three hired

men on the ranch. With her speed, strength and skill she could handle the sheep with deftness and ease.

Because of this smooth, harmonious, eager cooperation between us, the entire livestock operation prospered and flourished. The sheep were handled efficiently and with a minimum of disturbance. My own work was made much easier, lighter and more joyous. Lass herself was a totally fulfilled companion who reveled in all her responsibilities.

I sometimes thought of our overall relationship as a triad of triumph between master, friend and flock—all of it possible because of the loving cooperation of a beautiful border collie.

Reflecting on this happy association we enjoyed at "Fairwinds," I have often thought this is precisely the relationship Christ desires with us. It is bound to be one of the most profound and passionate longings of His love for us. More than anything else in all the world He wants me to be His companion, His coworker, His friend in helping to tend His flock.

This is really the essence of that entire final discourse He shared with His eleven disciples just before His death. It is recorded for us in great, authentic detail by John the Beloved in his Gospel, chapters 14, 15, 16 and 17. Any person who wishes to know and grasp the true meaning of "love for God" should read, mark and meditate over those superb insights.

Love for the Master is not some sweet, sentimental emotion that sweeps over the soul in moments of special piety. Love for Christ is a deliberate setting of the will to carry out His commands at any cost. It is the fixed attitude of heart that decides to do His will at all times. It is the desire and delight of accomplishing our Father's highest purposes, no matter how challenging.

The end result of such conduct for a Christian is to bring sweet satisfaction to the great Good Shepherd of his soul. Because of such bold and singleminded service we sense His approval of our behavior. We sense and know of a surety that we are loved and appreciated. We are His friends. And the ultimate end is that others benefit; others are blessed; others are cared for.

Jesus Himself put it this way:

"This is my commandment. That ye love one another, as I have loved you.

103

down his life for his friends. Ye are my friends, if ye do whatsoever I command you!"

(John 15:12–14).

As a simple footnote to this remarkable disclosure, it should be pointed out emphatically that "to lay down one's life" for another means to put the interests and wishes of others ahead of one's own. It implies that to obey Christ and carry out His intentions is ten times more desirable than "doing my own thing."

It is one thing to put this down with pen and paper. It is not a difficult statement to read from the written page. But it is the toughest lesson any of us can learn to live out in our daily duties.

In our highly permissive society, where the so-called "me" generation is encouraged to be so self-centered and so self-preoccupied, the call to obey Christ and comply with His commands cuts across our culture and our cynical conduct.

It simply is not normal nor natural for most of us to "love" God or "love" others in the drastic discipline of a laid-down life. We are a selfish, self-serving people. And when called upon to serve others we feel insulted. We have the strange, worldly idea that to be of lowly service is to be "used" or "abused."

Yet God, very God, in Christ came among us in lowly service. He came to minister to us. He came to give Himself to us. And so, because He first "loved" us, we in turn are to be willing and ready to "love" Him and others (see John 3:16–17 and 1 John 3:16–17).

As the years went by at "Fairwinds," I saw in ever-increasing clarity what Jesus meant when He spoke so often of His love for us and our love for Him. I began to understand a little the true implications and demands of a "laid-down life."

Continuously I was giving myself to Lass. I gave her my strength, my attention, my affection, my care, my loyalty, my friendship, my very life.

She in turn reciprocated this outpouring by giving back to me her vitality, her vigor, her enthusiasm, her spontaneous cooperation, her love, her loyalty.

Together all the benefits of this beautiful relationship were then poured out upon the flock. Our mutual energies and expertise were spent in caring for the sheep in happy comradeship.

105

It would be wonderful if this sheep dog story could just suddenly end here on this noble note. But it cannot. For, to be true to the tale, to be true to Lass, and to be true to life itself, it must be told that there were some disappointing interludes.

LESSONS FROM A SHEEP DOG

There were times, not many of them, but serious occasions, on which Lass did "break faith." There were days when she did not "stay" steadfast. There were distractions that came along which drew her away from her line of duty. Love, so betrayed, demands discipline to be restored.

There were grievous interludes both for her, for me and for the flock. To correct her and to mend the breach between us there had to be severe discipline. This was not easy or pleasant either for the dog or me. But it was absolutely essential for all of us.

I loved Lass far too much ever to let her revert back to her old, wretched life style. I was too fond of her to allow her to waste her energies for naught. She was far too precious ever to let her just pursue her own pointless ways. She was made for great things. She was intended for lofty service. So both of us would have to suffer to set her straight.

This is not an easy part of the story to tell.

Discipline is never pleasant.

The correction that comes with love causes pain both for the administrator and the recipient.

Many of us prefer to push it all aside. We would rather just wink at the wrongs. We find it easier to simply brush bad behavior to one side, acting as if it did not matter.

Love and Discipline

But true love demands discipline.

If we really care, we must correct.

If there is to be progress it comes at the cost of pain.

If there is to be mutual trust, integrity and loyalty again, then it must involve some suffering for us to learn this lesson, and learn it well.

It was not easy to punish Lass.

After all, she was my friend.

It demanded self-discipline on my part for me to insist that she perform properly, up to her full potential.

For years we had been joyous companions.

So it hurt me to have to discipline her.

I suffered as much as she suffered.

But for the benefit of us all it had to happen.

For the greater good of everyone involved she had to be chastened.

To correct her conduct with stern words or a severe reprimand or even a sharp slap made her draw back with reproach.

Her bright eyes would fill with foreboding.

She would lay back her ears with remorse.

She would crouch low, her tail drawn down between her legs, in a hangdog posture.

For a few moments there was a distinct coolness, a sense of alienation, a distance between us. This was a tense interlude both for me and her. She knew full well she had failed, and she knew I was far from satisfied with her performance.

I never allowed these interludes of discipline to drag on or last long. Correction came swiftly, it came surely, yet it was over in short order.

Then I would call her to me quietly. I would speak to her again softly in reassuring tones. "Lass, it's all over!" I would hold her close, rub her chest, run my hands over her head. "We're friends, all is well!"

Her eyes would begin to sparkle again as she looked up into my face. Sometimes she would reach out to lick my cheek with her tongue. Her body would quiver and she would begin to move her tail with pleasure.

Suddenly she would burst out of my embrace to go racing around on the grass in a wide circle, then come leaping back into my open, waiting arms. She was totally ecstatic, deliriously happy to be held and hugged again.

The strict discipline had brought total restoration of confidence and trust between us. We were fond and loyal friends again. Her highest good had been served. The best interests of all of us had been preserved.

Love and Discipline

For me as a man the entire area of God's discipline of my personal life was best learned from Lass. Through such examples I came to understand implicitly what my Master's intentions are for me during those times in life when He corrects my conduct.

As the Spirit of God makes so abundantly clear in Hebrews 12:6–11, "For whom the Lord loveth He chasteneth . . . (disciplines) . . . . Now no chastening for the present seemeth to be joyous, but grievous: nevertheless afterward it yieldeth the peaceable fruit of righteousness unto them which are exercised thereby."

For the last thirty years or more there has been prominent in the church, and among most preachers and teachers, an unbalanced and unfortunate overemphasis upon the "love of God." There has been a universal tendency to teach that Christ is so compassionate, so caring, so kind that He does not discipline us for our wrongdoing. There is the false impression now abroad that any old thing can go on, that God will simply forgive and forget all about it.

This simply is not so.

There is a price to pay for our perverseness. There is a discipline we deserve for wrongdoing.

LESSONS FROM A SHEEP DOG

There is the Master's demand that we be faithful in service, serious in our responsibilities to Him and others.

We distort the true character of Christ if we assert that He will merely wink at wrong. He does not! We delude ourselves and do Him enormous disservice if we feel we can just fool around as His followers. We cannot—without paying the consequences of alienation. He is grieved when we deliberately disobey His commands and selfishly ignore His wishes, to "do our own thing."

When Peter, the big, burly fisherman betrayed his Master the night before His crucifixion, it took only one stabbing, searching look to shatter the man's soul. He went out into the darkness to break down in tears and remorse. In fiery, burning shame he was reduced from a rough, tough, cursing fellow to a soul-shattered penitent.

Yet marvel of marvels, this was the man so swiftly restored after the Master's resurrection. He was the servant spoken to with such reassurance beside the lake. "Peter—do you love Me?—Then feed My sheep!" Three times over in a triad of tenderness the bonds of trust, love and loyalty were reestablished between Jesus and His friend.

Like Lass we shrink back from the discipline of

God. We find it grievous. We would rather it was set aside.

It cannot be. It is for our best. It is for His benefit. It is for the eventual blessing of others whose lives we touch.

And when it is all over, the bonds of affection between Christ and ourselves are even stronger than before. For, strange as it may seem, instinctively, surely, deep within our own spirits we know we deserve discipline. We know the Master would not be true to Himself or to us if He simply let our misconduct slide into sinister selfishness.

He disciplines because He cares, because He loves, because He heals.

With this reassurance comes renewed joy. There is total restoration. There is sheer delight in once again doing His bidding.

LESSON 7

Available for Anything

Perhaps the most unforgettable lesson I learned from Lass can best be summed up in three words: AVAILABLE FOR ANYTHING. The realization that though she was only a dog, she exhibited this remarkable trait in all of our years together, was tremendously challenging.

This was a source of never-ending amazement to me, especially in view of her initial reluctance even to come when I called her. The complete metamorphosis she had undergone in her behavior was beautiful to observe.

In this story of our days at "Fairwinds" I have tried to convey to the reader some of the love, some of the loyalty, some of the excitement we shared as master and "friend." Yet out of all these varied experiences it was ultimately Lass who taught me best what it really means to be utterly abandoned to the Master's purposes. She showed me in her vibrant loving devotion what it costs to be always available for anything that needed to be done in the best interests of the ranch and flock.

This principle is best understood by recounting two entirely different types of duty she was expected to carry out.

The first had to do with what is called "gathering up" or "counting" sheep. Because of the very character of sheep—their helplessness, their susceptibility to disease, their easy vulnerability to predators, their tendency to become "cast" on their backs, unable to right themselves again—they must be ever under the owner's constant scrutiny.

By far the quickest and surest way to make certain all is well is for the sheepman to take a "count" every day. In this way he knows at once if every sheep is on its feet, feeding contentedly and free from harm.

116

I can recall so clearly the sense of foreboding that would sweep over me whenever I went into the pastures and found that one or several of the ewes or lambs was missing.

I can still sense the despair that flooded over me when I came out in the morning to discover that either a cougar or stray dogs had wrought havoc among the flock during the night. Dead sheep or torn lambs would lie strewn in the fields. And only an accurate count would determine the devastating losses.

On other occasions, especially in the tranquil autumn, when the flock were fat and flourishing on the fallen acorns, it was quite common for the choicest ewes to become "cast." Unable to get back on their feet, they would soon die unless I found them in time to turn them over.

It was always an ominous sign when the dark-winged buzzards soared and wheeled in the sky above our rough and tumbled terrain. Immediately I knew they were watching for a hapless sheep that might soon provide them with a gory banquet at its carcass.

So I would call Lass. "Well, girl, we'll have to gather up the sheep today!" She would race up to my side, eyes shining, tail in happy motion, eager to go anywhere, any time.

Some of our land lay in beautiful open fields with occasional clumps of trees scattered over it like a lovely English park. Other parts were wild

117

and rough, especially along the shoreline. Some of this was very rocky, with great granite outcroppings. Amid the boulders there were patches of wild roses, thorny blackberry tangles, old stumps, windfalls and down timber.

The sheep loved to work their way into these spots searching for stray patches of sweet grass, new shoots of shrubbery or other dainty herbs they relished. It was no easy thing to find all the flock in such difficult cut-over country. But this was an important part of the work entrusted to Lass.

I would literally send her in "blind" to fetch out every straggling, stray ewe and lamb. Because I could count I would know if any were missing. And because I was much taller than Lass I could see over and beyond the obstacles to determine where the sheep were scattered.

"Fetch them in, Lass!" I would command her. "Go out and bring them home!" Without hesitating an instant the beautiful collie would be gone, leaping over the windfalls, pushing through the undergrowth, running over the rough rocks.

It was tremendously stimulating to watch her work with such eager enthusiasm. She literally flung herself into the task until every sheep was turned up and brought out.

There was a severe cost to the dog in all of this. She would become very weary. Often when she came back to me her face would be scratched and torn by the cruel thorns of the rose and blackberry thickets. Her coat would be clogged with burs and debris. Sometimes the pads of her feet would be cut and lacerated with the sharp stones.

There was suffering involved.

Yet she went gladly, joyously, with happy abandon.

She knew I knew what I was doing. And all she desired was to be a dynamic part of the whole project. She never held back. Not once did she hesitate to hurl herself into the toughest tangle to gather up the flock.

Her utter and selfless abandonment to my wishes made an enormous impact upon me. In quiet moments of reverie I would often ask myself the soul-searching questions: "Am I this readily available to my Master? Am I as willing to fling myself into His work anywhere? Am I so devoted to Him? Does the matter of suffering ever deter me from duty?"

More often than not Lass put me to shame.

LESSONS FROM A SHEEP DOG

Reflecting seriously upon all of this I began to see clearly why it is that Christ calls us, as His coworkers, to go into tough places. Being His "friend" is no cozy guarantee that life will always be either easy or even agreeable. There are simply bound to be some difficult duties, some tough assignments, some severe suffering if we are to fully comply with His commands.

I never, ever sent Lass into hard places to hurt her. But I put her into challenging circumstances to save the sheep and benefit the ranch operation. And it was out of all these endeavors together that she gradually matured and developed into a magnificent worker with me.

All of us as God's people seem to shrink back from suffering. We are so often reluctant to undertake even the smallest assignment for the Master. We hesitate to call on difficult people. We hold back from speaking to strangers. We are reluctant to share our strength, energy, time or talents to touch others in trouble. We do not want to give ourselves freely for the good of others. We draw back from the distasteful or difficult situation where we might have to suffer a bit by our involvement in order that others might be saved. We simply shrink from service that could bring others out of life's tangles to the Master.

I saw all of this vividly as I worked with Lass. Her shining spirit, her eager enthusiasm, her glad abandonment to my wishes combined to form a highly polished mirror in which I clearly saw reflected all the flaws of my own character—the failings of my own conduct toward Christ.

God's gracious Spirit used the humble devotion and hearty service of that beautiful collie to break some of my own tough resistance to His will for me.

If she could be so instantly available for anything, any time, anywhere, so, surely, I could do as well for God.

Many of us fail to realize what a lofty, noble honor it is to be called "the friend of God." We are often not shown what a stirring challenge it is to be called to suffer with Him. We do not seem to see that amid all the varied vicissitudes of life He really does know what He is doing with us. He can grasp the whole scheme of things. He can see far beyond our lowly, finite view. He, and He alone, is utterly in command and control of every situation.

Then let us trust Him fully.

Let us follow Him fearlessly.

Let us fling ourselves with glad abandon into His enterprises.

This Lass did with me—even in the darkest night and most dangerous engagements. This was the second way in which she proved her loyalty to me.

As the years went by at "Fairwinds" our happy times together were also interspersed with challenging events that demanded extra determination for us to survive.

The most frequent were attacks from both cougars and stray dogs at night. We lived close to very wild country where there were forested hills and wilderness terrain. This was ideal territory for deer and cougar. From time to time the cunning panthers would come out of the dense forest and raid the flock.

To warn us of the predators' stealthy approach at night I put bells on the sheep. Every fourth ewe carried a small copper bell on a collar worn around her neck. If the sheep were startled in the dark they would leap to their feet and flee for their lives. The wild tinkle of the bells awakened me from sleep.

122

I would leap out of bed, grab my flashlight, take the well-worn .303 rifle that stood by the door, and dash out into the fields. One never knew whether the sheep were being molested by stray dogs, cougars or rustlers.

For where we lived, most of the ranchers kept

sheep and rustling had become quite common in our part of the country. Men in trucks would back up to a fence, cut the wire to make a wide opening, then send their trained dogs into the pastures to round up a bunch of sheep, driving them right into the truck to be hauled away.

As I left the house in the dark, Lass would instantly be at my side. No need to even call her. With experience she, too, had learned to listen for the alarmed jangle of sheep bells ringing when the flock fled. It was a totally different sound from the soft tinkle when the sheep were grazing contentedly in the moonlit pastures.

Leaping joyously beside me she would bound up in the dark and lick my hand as if to say, "Cheer up, Boss, this is a great adventure!" So off we would go side by side to see what the danger was.

It always surprised me how quickly the sheep knew and sensed that we had come to protect them. In a remarkable way they would soon start to relax. In a few moments they would begin to graze quietly again or even lie down peacefully in the pastures.

123

Yet in all of this there was real danger for both Lass and myself. Rustlers were not averse to shooting the rancher's dog. Nor were other marauding dogs slow to attack another strange dog in the dark. Even the presence of a panther on the prowl was enough to make us doubly alert to any danger.

But Lass seemed to revel in all of this excitement. Not once did I ever see her cringe from our night forays in fear. Not once did she ever decide she would rather remain in the cozy comfort of her kennel.

Some nights she and I would actually go out and spend the entire night keeping watch in the fields. I would rest quietly in the grass, the rifle over my knees.

She would lie crouched on guard beside me. Her head often rested on my lap, but her eyes never closed, her ears were ever alert for the faintest strange sound. If anything aroused her a deep growl would rumble in her chest and I would be ready with the rifle.

These were intimate interludes for both of us. We were in this thing together. It was the tough way to meet a tough challenge. We simply had to be on guard. There was no other way to keep watch. But because of it we were able to keep the sheep from danger and protect them from their predators.

The Lord used this dear dog to teach me still

another truth about Himself in the dark and difficult episodes in life. He is always there! He is fully alert and aware of the dangers abroad! He is not taken unawares! He spares Himself no pains to protect us from those who would imperil our lives!

It is well to remind ourselves often of the utter faithfulness of God to us. We are too prone to believe that He really is not with us, that He does not know what dangers confront us, that He is out of touch with things!

Lass helped me to understand that it is often in the darkest hour, during pressing danger, that the Master is closest to us.

He cares, and He cares profoundly. It is His presence which gives us peace. It is His nearness which gives us hope. It is His protection which gives us life.

Amid all this He enjoys our company. He loves to have us alongside. He, too, finds consolation in the eager, alert watchfulness of His friends. In the midst of our danger there is delight. In the face of the foe there is quiet watchfulness. We need not be alarmed or anxious.

He is here!

All is well between us! Bless His wondrous name!

W. PHILLIP KELLER was born in East Africa and trained as an agronomist. He has worked as an agricultural development specialist, wildlife photographer and naturalist, and has expressed his love for nature and its God in many bestsellers. Among his bestselling books are *A Gardener Looks at the Fruits of the Spirit*, *Wonder O' the Wind* (his autobiography), *Lessons from a Sheepdog* (also on film and cassette), and *A Shepherd Looks at Psalm 23*. He is a popular author, lecturer, photographer, lay speaker, agrologist and ecology consultant. Keller is a graduate of the University of Toronto and Brooks Institute of Photography in California. His writing emanates from personal in-depth study of God's Word, intense prayerful meditation, and the sharing of spiritual truth with groups of God's people in various countries. In addition to books, he is featured on such Life-Lifter cassettes as "Forgiveness—What It Is and What It Costs," "The Potter and the Clay," and "What It Means to Receive Christ."